PICTURE A COUNTRY

Russia

Henry Pluckrose

W

FRANKLIN WATTS

A Division of Grolier Publishing
NEW YORK • LONDON • HONG KONG • SYDNEY
DANBURY, CONNECTICUT

This is the Russian flag.

Photographic acknowledgements:

Cover: Hutchison Library t, Impact Photos br (above), AA Photo Library br (below).

Insides: AA Photo Libary pp. 18, 22; AKG London pp. 14-15, 26, 28, 29b; Axiom Photographic Agency p. 27 (Jim Holmes); Bryan and Cherry Alexander pp. 9, 11l, 13, 17; Colorific! pp. 11r (Black Star/Erica Lansner); Robert Harding pp. 8 (Charles O'Rear); Hutchison Library pp. 19 (A. Grachtchenkov), 24 (Igor Gavrilov); Impact Photos pp. 10 (Peter Arkell), 20 (Peter Arkell), 21 (Peter Arkell); Planet Earth Pictures pp. 16b, 16t; Popperfoto p. 25 (Dave Joiner); Russia and Republics Photo Library pp. 23, 29t (Mark Wadlow); Spectrum Colour Library pp. 12 (G.R. Richardson) 14.

All other photography Steve Shott.

Map by Julian Baker

Series editor: Rachel Cooke
Editor: Alex Young
Series designer: Kirstie Billingham
Picture research: Susan Mennell

First published in 1999 by Franklin Watts
First American edition 1999 by
Franklin Watts
A Division of Grolier Publishing
90 Sherman Turnpike
Danbury, CT 06816

Visit Franklin Watts on the Internet at:
http://publishing.grolier.com

Pluckrose, Henry Arthur.
    Russia / Henry Pluckrose.
        p. cm. -- (Picture a country)
    Includes index.
    Summary: A simple introduction to the geography, people, culture, and interesting sites of Russia.
    ISBN 0-531-14503-4
    1. Russia (Federation) --Juvenile literature. [1. Russia (Federation)] I. Title. II. Series: Pluckrose, Henry Arthur. Picture a country.
DS10.56.P58 1999
947--dc21   98-11686
                                                          CIP
                                                           AC

GROLIER
PUBLISHING

Contents

Where Is Russia?

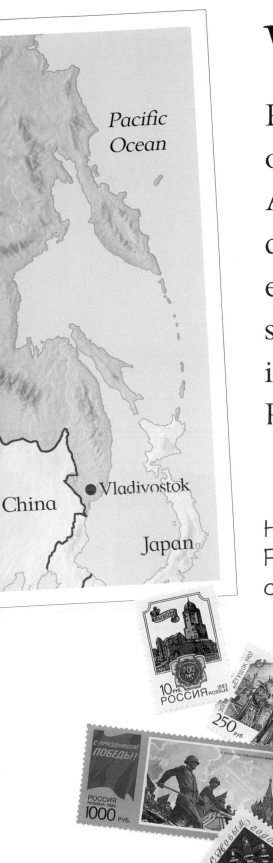

Russia is where the continents of Europe and Asia meet. The Arctic Ocean is to the north and the Pacific Ocean to the east. The Ural Mountains separate the part of Russia that is in Europe from the part of Russia that is in Asia.

Here are some Russian stamps and money.

Russian money is counted in rubles.

The Russian Landscape

Russia is the largest country in the world, so it has many different kinds of landscapes. There are mountains, deserts, and many rivers. There are also wide plains that stretch for thousands of miles.

These reindeer are grazing on the plains of the Yamal Peninsula in northwest Siberia.

In some parts of Russia, such as around the Black Sea, the weather is warm throughout the year. In other parts, for example in Siberia, the weather is dry and very cold.

The Russian People

People first came to live in the lands we call
Russia over 500 thousand years ago.
Today over 148 million people live in Russia.

These babushkas wearing fur hats are standing in a crowd in Moscow. "Babushka" is Russian for "grandmother".

Many different races live in Russia.

There are three main languages spoken in Russia — Tatar, Ukrainian, and Russian.

Where They Live

Most Russians live in cities in the European part of Russia. Many others, both in the west and the east of the country, live and work in small towns and countryside villages.

Some Russians have country houses called dachas.

The city of Nadym in Western Siberia is often covered in snow.

Most important towns and cities are in European Russia. But even in eastern Russia, there are large cities such as Nadym.

The Capital City

Moscow is the capital of Russia. Nearly 9 million people live there.

The river Moskva runs through the center of Moscow.

The Kremlin lies at the center of Moscow. It is a citadel with high walls. Inside there are churches and palaces.

The wall around the Kremlin is 2,200 feet (2,195 m) long.

Space Stations

The Russians are famous for exploring space with rockets, satellites, and space stations.

This man is in the MIR space station. Russian spacemen are called cosmonauts.

A worker struggles with a hose at a natural gas drilling rig in Siberia.

Factories across Russia make all kinds of things, from aircraft and cars to paper and textiles. Precious stones and metals are mined, as well as coal, natural gas, and oil.

Farming

Russian farmers grow many crops, including wheat, barley, fruit, and vegetables. They also keep cattle, sheep, goats, and chickens for meat.

These farmers are harvesting hay on Yelagin Island near St Petersburg.

The River Volga is a good place for fishermen to catch sturgeon.

Russian fishermen take their trawlers into the Arctic, Atlantic, and Pacific oceans. Sturgeon are caught in Lake Baikal and in many rivers. Sturgeon eggs (called caviar) are a favorite Russian food.

Home and School

In Russian towns and cities, families often live in high-rise apartment buildings. Russian children have to go to school until they are eighteen. Some continue their education by going to college.

Russian children do much the same things at school as you. These girls are in an art class.

These children are playing outside an apartment building in Moscow.

Russian Food

People in different parts of Russia enjoy different kinds of food. Wherever you go, soup (called borscht) is a favorite meal. Borscht can be made from almost anything — scraps of meat, beets, carrots, potatoes, tomatoes, onions, mushrooms, and cabbage.

Thin round pancakes called blini are often eaten with caviar.

A Russian vegetable market in Irkutsk in eastern Siberia

Kulibiaka — a pie filled with egg, meat, chicken, or cabbage — is another favorite meal and is often eaten on special occasions.

Out and About

Russian people enjoy music and dancing. The Bolshoi Ballet is one of the most famous ballet companies in the world.

These dancers are from the Bolshoi Ballet.

Russian Olympic gold medal winner Andrei Chemerkin lifts 108 kilograms (290 pounds).

Russians also enjoy all kinds of sports — track and field, basketball, soccer, volleyball, gymnastics, ice hockey, ice skating, swimming, and weightlifting.

Religion and Festivals

Many Russians are Russian Orthodox Christians. The Orthodox Church celebrates Christmas on January 7.

Ancient paintings called icons can be found in most Russian churches.

Many Russian churches are topped by "onion"-shaped domes.

Festivals and celebrations take place all over Russia throughout the year. Many of these festivals are religious, but there are also ceremonies to remember famous people and events from the past.

Visiting Russia

Many tourists go to Russia to see its famous art galleries or to watch the ballet or the opera.

The Winter Palace in St. Petersburg was home to Russia's royal family. It is now an art gallery.

Many tourists travel on the Trans-Siberian Railway. It takes about eight days to go from Moscow to Vladivostok.

Peter Fabergé was a famous Russian jeweler in the 1880s. He designed beautiful eggs for rich people to give as gifts. Today, you can see many of these precious eggs in Russian museums.

Index

About This Book

The last decade of the 20th century has been marked by an explosion in communications technology. The effect of this revolution upon the young child should not be underestimated. The television set brings a cascade of ever-changing images from around the world into the home, but the information presented is only on the screen for a few moments before the program moves on to consider some other issue.

Instant pictures, instant information do not easily satisfy young children's emotional and intellectual needs. Young children take time to assimilate knowledge, to relate what they already know to ideas and information that are new.

The books in this series seek to provide snapshots of everyday life in countries in different parts of the world. The images have been selected to encourage the young reader to look, to question, to talk. Unlike the TV picture, each page can be studied for as long as is necessary and subsequently returned to as a point of reference. For example, the Russian climate might be compared with their own, or a discussion might develop about the ways in which food is prepared and eaten in a country whose culture and customs are different from their own.

The comparison of similarity and difference is the recurring theme in each of the titles in this series. People in different lands are superficially different. Where they live (the climate and terrain) obviously shapes the sort of houses that are built, but people across the world need shelter; coins may look different, but in each country people use money.

At a time when the world seems to be shrinking, it is important for children to be given the opportunity to focus upon those things that are common to all the peoples of the world. By exploring the themes touched upon in the book, children will begin to appreciate that there are strands in the everyday life of human beings that are universal.